DATE DUE

Ollhoff, Jim.

616.9   **What are germs?**

OLL

A History of Germs

WHAT ARE GERMS?

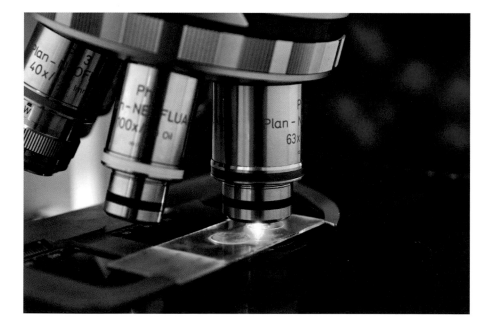

 By Jim Ollhoff

VISIT US AT
WWW.ABDOPUBLISHING.COM

Published by ABDO Publishing Company, 8000 West 78th Street, Suite 310, Edina, MN 55439. Copyright ©2010 by Abdo Consulting Group, Inc. International copyrights reserved in all countries. No part of this book may be reproduced in any form without written permission from the publisher. ABDO & Daughters™ is a trademark and logo of ABDO Publishing Company.

Printed in the United States.

♻ PRINTED ON RECYCLED PAPER

Editor: John Hamilton
Graphic Design: Sue Hamilton
Cover Design: John Hamilton
Cover Photo: iStockphoto
Interior Photos and Illustrations: AP-Pgs 23 & 28; Centers for Disease Control and Prevention-Pgs 20, 21, & 24; Corbis-pg 25; The Granger Collection-pg 6; iStockphoto-pgs 1, 3, 4, 5, 10, 12, 15, & 19; Jupiterimages-pgs 7, 15, 16, 17, 18, & 26; Photo Researchers-pgs 6, 8, 9, 11, 13, 14, 22, 26 & 27; and Wikimedia-pg 29.

Library of Congress Cataloging-in-Publication Data

Ollhoff, Jim, 1959-
  What are germs? / Jim Ollhoff.
    p. cm. – (A history of germs)
  Includes index.
  ISBN 978-1-60453-502-0
  1. Germ theory of disease–Juvenile literature. 2. Bacteria–Juvenile literature. I. Title.

  RB153.O45 2010
  616.9'041–dc22

                                2008055064

CONTENTS

WHAT ARE GERMS? ☣

They are everywhere. They live on your skin. They are in your mouth. They are in your nostrils, on your hair, and on your clothes. Germs live on the pages of this book, on the floor, on the ceiling, and in your intestines. Germs are everywhere.

Germs live on the top of Mount Everest, and in the lowest ocean trenches. They live in the steam vents of Old Faithful in Yellowstone National Park. They live under glaciers in Alaska, and they live in the sands of the Sahara Desert. A shovelful of dirt may have a half-million different kinds of germs. Not a half-million germs. A half-million different *kinds* of germs. But, the truth is, we couldn't live without germs.

A more scientific name for germs is *microorganisms*, or *microbes* for short. A microbe is usually a living thing too small to be seen by the naked eye. Some microbes cause disease and death. Other microbes help us live.

Microbes help you digest food. Microbes help create vitamins. They break down animal waste into nutrients that plants need to grow. Bacteria on your skin fight off dangerous pests. Some microbes can even destroy toxic chemicals, making it safe for other life.

The scientific name for germs is microorganism, or microbes for short.

Microbes are often studied under the eye of powerful microscopes.

A shovelful of dirt may contain half a million kinds of germs.

Microbes are very resilient little creatures. They can go dormant, as if they are in suspended animation. Centuries after being frozen in a glacier, some microbes can be revived. Some can even resist extreme heat by changing themselves into spores and floating away.

GOOD GERMS AND BAD GERMS

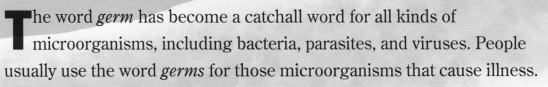

The word *germ* has become a catchall word for all kinds of microorganisms, including bacteria, parasites, and viruses. People usually use the word *germs* for those microorganisms that cause illness.

Bacteria were probably first seen by the Dutch scientist Antoni van Leeuwenhoek in 1683. But it was a long time before scientists understood the function of bacteria. It wasn't until the late 1800s when the great scientists Louis Pasteur and Robert Koch realized that some bacteria actually caused illnesses. It was probably Pasteur himself who first used the word "germ."

Louis Pasteur

Robert Koch

Sometimes people are afraid of bacteria, and they go overboard with cleanliness.

Today, we know that some microbes are good for us, and provide a great many services. They make yogurt and cheese by curdling milk. Out in the forest, microbes chew on plants and leaves, leaving behind fertile soil. Some kinds of microbes in your mouth protect you from other, more harmful bacteria. Microbes in your intestines break down food so that your body can use the nutrients.

Sometimes people are afraid of bacteria, and they go overboard with cleanliness. In fact, some homes are actually *too* clean. When children live in houses that are too clean, they become more prone to some illnesses, like asthma and Crohn's disease. The human body needs to be exposed to bacteria so that the immune system can learn to fight off invaders. If a body is not exposed to bacteria, its immune system may become lazy, and it doesn't learn how to fight.

In homes that are too clean, kids may be prone to such illnesses as asthma.

KINDS OF GERMS

There are different kinds of creatures that fall into the category of microbes, or germs. This book will focus on bacteria, viruses, fungi, and protozoa.

Bacteria are one-celled microbes. They have many kinds of shapes. Some bacteria are round, others are shaped like sausages. Some have tails, called flagella, that help them swim. Some form spores, which make them airborne and more resistant to high temperatures.

There are billions of kinds of bacteria, and the vast majority of them are neither helpful nor harmful to humans. However, there are a few nasty ones. *Salmonella* is sometimes found in contaminated meat. When the *Salmonella* cells die, they produce a toxin that causes nausea, fever, and vomiting. *Escherichia coli*, usually called *E. coli*, is another foodborne bacteria that can cause digestive problems.

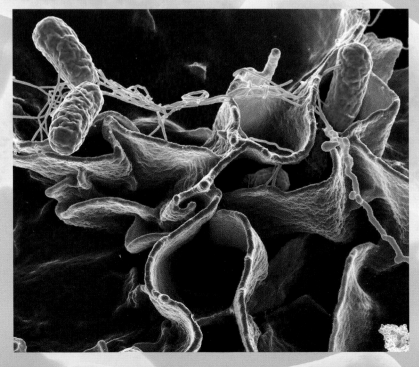

Salmonella bacteria (green) can cause food poisoning when they are eaten in contaminated food.

Viruses are another kind of germ, but they are very different from bacteria. Viruses are not technically alive, and so are not true microbes. A virus is a collection of DNA. When a virus gets into the body, it inserts its DNA into a living cell, and then tricks the cell into making more viruses.

Viruses are extremely small, much smaller than bacteria. They couldn't be seen with early microscopes. It wasn't until 1892 that viruses were discovered by Russian scientist Dmitry Ivanovsky.

Russian scientist Dmitry Ivanovsky discovered viruses in 1892.

The common cold is spread by a virus. Influenza, polio, HIV, and hemorrhagic fevers are just a few of the many diseases that are caused by viruses.

Cleaning the kitchen counter or washing hands can kill harmful germs. When people cover their mouth when they cough, or sneeze into a tissue, they help reduce the spread of germs.

The growth on old bread are fungi. Fungi make up a huge number of microbes.

Fungi (the plural of fungus) make up a huge number of microbes. The black goo that shows up on bathroom walls is a fungus. The growths that appear on sides of trees in the forests are fungi. Mushrooms, both the edible and poisonous kinds, are in the fungus family. The green growth that appears on old bread, as well as the yeast that makes bread rise, are fungi. People always have fungi on their feet. When it gets out of control, it gets red and itchy, and is known as athlete's foot. Many antibiotics are made from fungi.

The largest living organism in the world is a fungus. A humongous *Armillaria bulbosa* was discovered in Michigan in 1992. It lives under the soil, and is between 1,000 and 10,000 years old. It has spread itself over at least 37 acres (15 ha), and weighs about 100 tons (91 metric tons).

Giardia protozoa are found in lakes and rivers.

Protozoa are another kind of microbe. There are more than 65,000 known kinds of protozoa. They convert sunlight to food, like plants, but they move under their own power, like animals. They seem to be halfway between plants and animals. When people drink water from lakes or rivers, they can ingest a protozoa called *Giardia*, which causes diarrhea, vomiting, and fever.

People may get very sick if they drink unclean water.

GERMS IN YOUR HOME

Microbes are everywhere in your house, of course. But where are the most dangerous germs found? The worst place for germs isn't the bathroom.

The worst place for germs is the kitchen. There are two reasons for this: First, people spend a lot of time there, transferring germs from one place to another with their hands. Second, it's where food products are, and uncooked food often contains harmful bacteria.

Uncooked food often contains harmful bacteria.

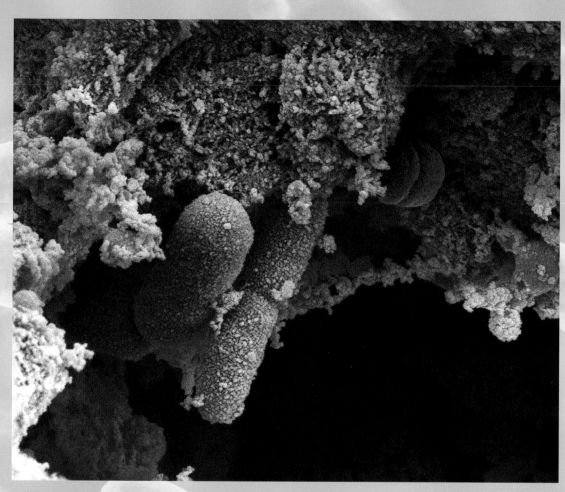

Undercooked beef showing *E. coli* bacteria.

Germs love places that are wet and warm. So, kitchen sponges and dirty dishrags are good places to find germs. Since sponges and dishrags often don't dry out, they become a good place for germs to breed. Kitchen cutting boards are also usually full of bacteria, because people often don't clean them very well. Cutting uncooked meat on a board will leave lots of germs. The knife that cuts the uncooked meat will also be contaminated with germs. It can transfer those germs if it touches something else. Cooking the meat will typically kill the germs, but the juices of uncooked meat can be a treasure trove of harmful bacteria.

The laundry room is another germy place. Lots of dirty, soiled clothes sitting in warm piles in a dark room—a very inviting place for bacteria.

The bathroom also has germs because the shower makes the room wetter than others. Bacteria like moist places. In public bathrooms, the germiest places are the handles of the toilets. The handles are always wet from condensation, and people touch them constantly. Surprisingly, the toilet seat itself isn't too bad. It would be difficult to catch a germ from a toilet seat.

Office areas and homework areas are often very germy, simply because we don't think to clean them very often. Usually, we don't remember to clean our desk until we start sticking to it. But keyboards, telephones, and other areas can be germy because we touch those areas often. Most germs are transferred from place to place on our hands, so whatever we touch a lot becomes germy.

Most germs are transferred from place to place on people's hands.

Are Dogs Mouths Clean?
Are Cats Mouths Dirty?

Some people say that dogs have germ-free mouths. Others say cats have terribly germy mouths, just waiting to give people a dangerous infection. Are these statements true? The answer is no.

Dogs have oral bacteria, just like humans. But they are different kinds of bacteria. Germs that make dogs sick typically don't make humans sick. The bigger problem is that dogs have a charming habit of licking their own urinary and anal areas. This can put fecal matter in their mouths, which can transfer when they lick a person's face. Fecal matter often carries harmful bacteria.

Cats don't have mouths that are more germy. However, their bites are indeed more dangerous than dogs. Cats have teeth that are very long and narrow. So, when they bite a person, they can make puncture wounds that push bacteria deep into the tissue. The tissue then closes up around the narrow puncture, so it's impossible to wash the bacteria out of the wound. Cat bites can lead to dangerous infections, but it's because of the shape of the teeth, not the number of bacteria in their mouths.

HOW GERMS SPREAD

Fred has a bad cold. He sneezes, covering his mouth. Some of the germs that were in Fred's sinuses fly out and land on Fred's hand. Fred gets a drink at the drinking fountain, and his hand touches the handle, leaving behind some germs.

Richard comes along and wants a drink, so he grabs the handle of the drinking fountain. Now, the germs get on Richard's hand. Later, Richard has an itch on his nose. He rubs his nose, and some of the germs from his hand get into his nose, where they embed in the soft, moist tissues. A few days later, the germs have grown and multiplied, and now Richard has a bad cold.

This is how most germs are spread. Fred sneezed, and while he was careful to cover his mouth, he didn't wash his hands afterward. So, Fred carries some of those germs on his hands. That's how most germs are transmitted—on people's hands. A good handwashing with soap and water would have killed most of the germs on Fred's hands, but since he didn't wash his hands, he became a carrier.

Fred began to leave germs on almost everything he touched—desks, doorknobs, and drinking fountain handles. Germs can live for a little while outside the body, especially if the place is moist and warm, and there is a tiny bit of bodily fluid in which the germs live. In this case, the drinking fountain handle was a perfect place for germs to live, because the handle was wet with condensation.

So Richard comes along and touches the handle, getting germs on his hand. By itself, this isn't bad. Germs can't get through Richard's skin. The problem is when Richard touches his nose or rubs his eyes. Germs love the soft, moist tissues of the eyes and nose. That's how most germs get into a body.

So, if Richard had washed his hands, he would have killed the germs. But, he touched his nose, giving himself a cold. Children and youth touch their faces about 100 times every hour. That's a lot of opportunity to spread germs.

So, if germs are everywhere, how can we avoid them? Should we all buy hazardous materials suits? Fortunately, no. First, the vast majority of germs are not harmful. Second, while it's true that germs are everywhere, the problem isn't the existence of germs. The problem is when we take the germs and put them into our nose or eyes.

Ninety-nine percent of the problem can be solved with two simple techniques: First, try not to touch your face when you are out among other people. Second, wash your hands often. Hands should be washed with soap and water, for at least 15 to 30 seconds, especially in the area around your fingernails. Anti-bacterial soap isn't necessary—regular soap will work just fine. The problem is that most people don't wash their hands very effectively. They barely touch the soap, and then rinse their hands under water for only a few seconds. This does little to kill germs. Medical studies show that people who effectively wash their hands six times a day will have a lot less illnesses than other people.

There are ways other than buying a hazardous materials suit to protect yourself from harmful germs.

EFFECTIVE HANDWASHING

7 Steps to Prevent the Spread of Germs

Turn on water to a comfortable temperature and moisten hands and wrists.

Apply a generous portion of liquid soap.

Generate a heavy lather and wash well for approx. 15 seconds . Clean between fingers, nail beds, under fingernails and backs of hands

Rinse well under running water, keeping hands low in sink to prevent splashing.

Hold hands so that water flows from the wrist to fingertips.

Dry hands completely with clean paper towels.

Use the paper towel to turn off the faucet so your hands remain clean.

People who effectively wash their hands at least six times a day will have a lot less illnesses than other people.

DEADLY DISEASES IN HISTORY

One of the worst diseases in history was smallpox. Caused by a virus, this disease was fatal for about one-third of the people who got sick. Europeans unknowingly brought smallpox to North America in the 1500s. Smallpox nearly wiped out many Native American peoples, who had no immunity to this disease. As terrible as smallpox was, it also led to one of the greatest success stories in modern medicine. Aggressive worldwide vaccination programs in the 1960s and 1970s wiped it off the face of the earth.

A 1974 photo of a boy from Bengal, India, with smallpox. By 1980, thanks to aggressive vaccinations, smallpox was declared dead.

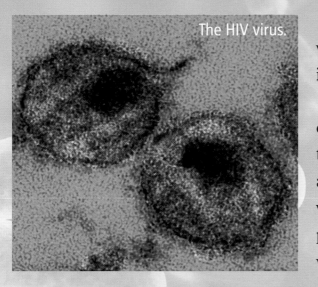
The HIV virus.

The human immunodeficiency virus (HIV) can lead to acquired immunodeficiency syndrome (AIDS). HIV is spread through certain bodily fluids, and attacks the immune system. Despite advanced anti-viral drugs, the virus kills two to three million people each year around the world.

HIV kills 2-3 million people each year.

An *anopheles* mosquito may carry the malaria parasite.

Malaria is a disease that is caused by a parasite in the saliva of mosquitoes. The disease is preventable and curable, but in many places of the world, people cannot afford the expensive medication. Malaria is almost unknown in North America, but common in central Africa. The disease kills more than one million people each year, mostly children.

Malaria is curable, but many can't afford the medication.

Fleas sometimes infect their human hosts with the plague virus *Yersinia Pestis*.

The bubonic plague was a deadly killer throughout history. One of the worst epidemics was in Europe in the years 1347 to 1351. About one-third of the population of Western Europe died in what was called the "Black Death." This caused great economic and political upheaval.

The bubonic plague killed millions of people.

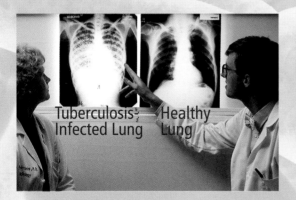

Tuberculosis Infected Lung   Healthy Lung

Tuberculosis is a disease caused by a bacterium that usually attacks the lungs. Signs of tuberculosis have been found in the bodies of 3,000-year-old Egyptian mummies. In 1944, the first antibiotic effective against tuberculosis was created, and at one time scientists hoped to stamp it out forever. However, the bacterium has become resistant to many antibiotics. Today, it takes a cocktail of several antibiotics, given over a period of months, to kill the bacteria. Tuberculosis has made a big comeback in areas where people can't afford medicines. It also takes advantage of people whose immune systems are weak, such as those people with HIV. Worldwide, about two million people die each year from tuberculosis.

Sanitation engineers may have saved more lives than doctors in the last century or two. Clean water, public restrooms, and sewer systems have prevented the loss of life that once was common. There are several bacteria that cause life-threatening diarrhea, usually from drinking impure water. These "diarrheal diseases" include cholera, amoebic dysentery, and typhoid. People who get these diseases lose fluid so quickly that they die of dehydration.

As early as 1832, doctors realized that they should give fluids to people suffering from these germs. Today, in North America, these problems can usually be treated with medication before they become life threatening. However, in other parts of the world today, more than one billion people don't have clean water to drink. These sicknesses kill more than two million people each year.

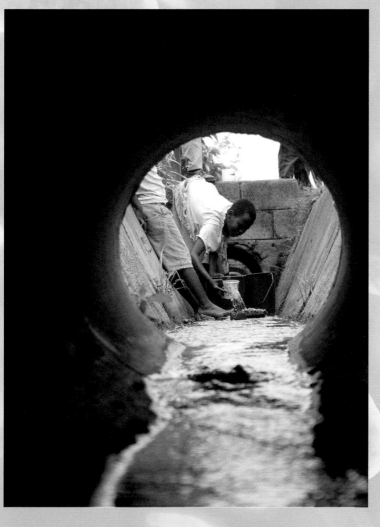

People collect rain water from a roadside drainage system in Harare, Zimbabwe, in 2009. However, the unclean water has caused an outbreak of cholera in the country.

GERM-FIGHTING ORGANIZATIONS

The United States is served by the Centers for Disease Control and Prevention (CDC). This organization began in 1946, taking malaria control out of the hands of the military. One of the CDC's first tasks was to kill the mosquitoes in the United States that spread malaria. Today, the CDC provides leadership in public health and control of infectious diseases. When there's a medical emergency, such as the early phase of an epidemic or a disease outbreak, the CDC quickly responds. The CDC has 14,000 employees in more than 50 countries. The Public Health Agency of Canada provides a similar function as the CDC.

One of the CDC buildings in Atlanta, Georgia.

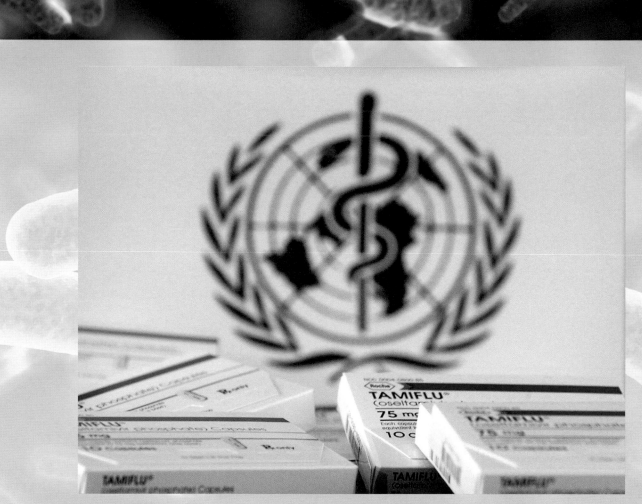

In May 2009, the World Health Organization distributed medication in Mexico City, Mexico, to battle against the city's H1N1 flu outbreak. The WHO monitors outbreaks of various kinds of diseases and looks for causes.

The World Health Organization (WHO) is an agency of the United Nations. It helps to coordinate and monitor information, as well as sponsor programs to treat diseases. The WHO monitors outbreaks of various kinds of diseases and looks for causes. The WHO helps to develop and distribute medicines to areas that need it. Today, public health organizations need to network together and constantly communicate, and the WHO helps to serve that purpose. It was the WHO that helped organize the global eradication of smallpox, declaring the disease wiped out in 1980.

CURRENT CONCERNS ABOUT GERMS

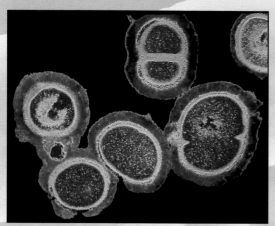

A strain of staphylococcus bacteria resistant to antibiotic drugs.

Doctors today are very concerned about antibiotic-resistant germs. These are germs that have evolved and changed so that older antibiotics and medicines are not as effective. In many countries, antibiotics are overused, which makes it easy for germs to become resistant. Tuberculosis and malaria are two of the illnesses that are showing increasing resistance to medicine.

New Medicines

Can scientists develop new medicines fast enough? Antibiotics kill bacteria, and antiviral medications slow down or stop viruses. As the germs change, new medicines must be developed.

New Germs

New germs emerge occasionally in the human population, and some are very serious. One example is severe acute respiratory syndrome (SARS), which is caused by a virus. In late 2002, the disease appeared in southern China. By 2003, more than 8,000 people became sick with breathing problems, and 774 died. Quick action to quarantine people and track their contacts helped contain the disease. By 2004, the disease stopped as quickly as it emerged. The World Health Organization declared the disease eradicated in 2005.

The SARS virus.

Another recent new disease is from the Ebola virus, which was first identified in 1976. Almost 2,000 cases have been reported in a variety of outbreaks. More than 1,200 deaths have occurred, making it a very deadly virus. Ebola is a terrible disease, causing people to bleed to death internally.

Politics and Disease

Polio, which can cause temporary or permanent paralysis, has been eliminated in North America. However, it remains a crippling disease in other countries in the world. It is hoped that polio will be eradicated someday soon.

Decades ago, people feared polio. It could cripple a child suddenly, without warning. Aggressive vaccinations have eliminated the disease in North America. Today, the virus only exists in a few countries of the world. The World Health Organization believes polio could be eradicated from the earth in a few years, but only if political leaders make it one of their top priorities.

Malaria, too, is a curable, preventable disease that still kills one million children in Africa every year. Do the world's leaders have the will to spend the resources to end malaria?

Bioterrorism

Many fear that terrorists will find a way to develop some kind of biological weapon of terror. Some fear that terrorists could find a way to weaponize Ebola, smallpox, or some other germ. While this would take a tremendous amount of technical knowledge, some people are still concerned.

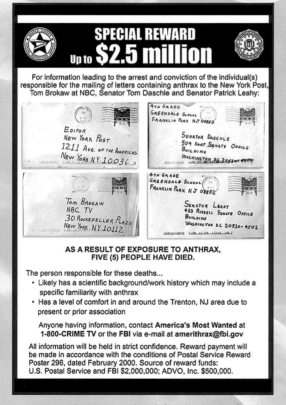

In 2001, the FBI asked for help to find whoever sent anthrax through the mail.

In September 2001, several letters were mailed to United States senators and news media offices. These letters contained anthrax spores, which caused sickness and killed five people. Since these attacks began only a week after the terrorist attacks of September 11, many people assumed that foreign terrorists had created them. It wasn't until 2008 that the FBI tracked down the source of the anthrax letters. The FBI believed that the letters came from Bruce Ivins, a United States scientist who worked in anthrax research for the military. He took his own life shortly before the authorities were about to arrest him. He was a psychologically troubled man, and it is unclear how he worked for so long at a government facility.

GLOSSARY

ANTIBIOTICS

A class of medicines that kill harmful bacteria in the body. Antibiotics only kill bacteria, not viruses.

ANTIVIRALS

A class of medicines that will slow or stop the progress of viruses in the body.

BACTERIA

A one-celled organism.

DNA

DNA is short for the scientific term Deoxyribonucleic Acid. In living things, DNA is the material inside the center of every cell that forms genes. This material is inherited from an individual's parents.

EPIDEMIC

When a disease spreads across a wide region. For example, the disease smallpox was very contagious and could easily be caught by those nearby, in time spreading over large areas.

FUNGI

Plural of fungus. A class of plant-like microbes.

MICROBES

A word abbreviated from microorganism.

MICROORGANISMS

A word to describe the variety of one-celled and microscopic life.

PARASITE

An organism that resides in or on a host, usually doing damage to the host.

PROTOZOA

A class of microbes.

QUARANTINE

The practice of keeping infected people separate, so they won't infect healthy people.

VACCINATION

The process of giving a person a dead or weakened form of a germ (vaccine), so that the immune system will recognize it and give the person an immunity to the germ.

VIRUS

A class of microbes, not technically alive, but active in hijacking a cell and forcing the cell to reproduce the viruses.

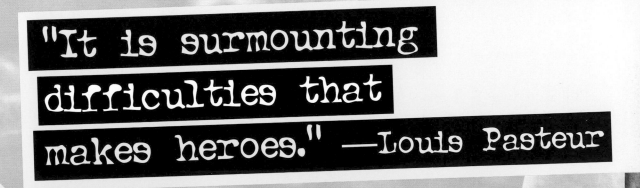

"It is surmounting difficulties that makes heroes." —Louis Pasteur

INDEX